D1623876

LAWYERS

· ·

AND OTHER REPTILES II

THE APPEAL

LAWYERS

AND OTHER REPTILES II

THE APPEAL

JESS M. BRALLIER

CB

CONTEMPORARY BOOKS

A TRIBUNE COMPANY

Library of Congress Cataloging-in-Publication Data

Brallier, Jess M.
     Lawyers and other reptiles II : the appeal / Jess
M. Brallier.
        p.   cm.
    ISBN 0-8092-3319-3
    1. Lawyers—Humor.   2. Lawyers—Quotations.
I. Title.
PN6231.L4B685   1996
808.88′2—dc20   95-48210
                                    CIP

Published by Contemporary Books, Inc.
Two Prudential Plaza, Chicago, Illinois 60601-6790
Manufactured in the United States of America
International Standard Book Number: 0-8092-3319-3
10   9   8   7   6   5   4   3   2   1

INTRODUCTION

· ·

Some time ago I compiled a collection of lawyer jokes, quotes, and anecdotes entitled *Lawyers and Other Reptiles*. A publisher agreed to take it on . . . which delighted me. The book has sold, to date, nearly 200,000 copies . . . which surprises me. At the end of that book I suggested readers send me further jokes, quotes, and anecdotes for another such collection (any reader whose submission was used would be awarded a free copy of the new book). I have received, to date, 1,294 letters . . . which astounds me.

So here it is, the long-awaited (well, four years anyway) sequel—*Lawyers and Other Reptiles II: The Appeal*, at the core of which are selected contributions of those 1,294 readers. Sure, most of you who wrote are not going to get a free book (85 will) because either I had already gathered your suggested tidbit or your submission failed to reach my mail box before somebody else's (the old "first come, first selected" process). A list of contributors can be found near the end of this book.

For those of you whose submission was not chosen, I wish you better luck on the third compilation, *Lawyers and Other Reptiles III: The Rebuttal* (see page 107). Meanwhile—because my personal lawyer is standing outside my office door with a stack of legal bills which I need to pay ASAP—please continue to encourage friends, family, and colleagues to purchase many copies of these books. Thanks!

Two acquaintances were walking down the street. One said to the other, "Hey, I heard a good lawyer joke."

"But I'm a lawyer," protested the other.

"Oh," the first replied. "Well, I can tell it to you slowly."

In July 1993, soon after the publication of *Lawyers and Other Reptiles*, the president of the California State Bar denounced lawyer-bashing, called for a moratorium on lawyer jokes, and proposed that lawyers should be afforded special protection under the law.

"The differences between lawyer jokes and attorney jokes is about fifty dollars an hour."

—*Milton Berle*

St. Peter was waiting at the Pearly Gates to determine the fate of three heart attack victims. He asked the first man, "What caused your heart attack?"

"My wife caught me in bed with another woman."

"I'm sorry," said St. Peter, "but you'll have to go down the elevator to eternal damnation."

The same question was asked of the second person, who replied, "The IRS caught me cheating on my income tax." St. Peter directed him to the same elevator.

Then the third person was also asked, "What caused your heart attack?" He replied, "I got my lawyer's bill." Whereupon he was immediately escorted by angels through the Pearly Gates to Heaven.

"The penalty for laughing in the courtroom is six months in jail: if it were not for this penalty, the jury would never hear the evidence."

—*H. L. Mencken*

QUESTION: What do you get when you cross a snake with a lawyer?
ANSWER: Incest.

A piece of paper, blown by the wind into a law court may in the end only be drawn out again by two oxen.

—*Chinese proverb*

A lawyer and a carpenter were at the beach, walking along the water's edge, when they passed by a beautiful, shapely, and scantily clad young woman.

"Boy, I'd like to screw her," said the carpenter.

"Out of what?" said the lawyer.

In Page Smith's 1962 biography (of President and attorney) *John Adams*, the author notes that Adams's own neighbors in Braintree (Massachusetts) were especially suspicious "of lawyers as a class—one might even say a caste. They were at best, in the view of most of Braintree, a necessary evil. With their sharp ways, with their intricate and obscure writs and pleadings, their forms and formalities, their often condescending manners, they could trick a man out of his shirt or out of his farm before he knew it."

Posting in the kitchen of a lawyer's office:

I'm going to prove you innocent even if it takes every penny you stole.

"The one great principle of the English law is, to make business for itself. There is no other principle distinctly, certainly, and consistently maintained through all its narrow turnings. Viewed by this light it becomes a coherent scheme, and not the monstrous maze the laity are apt to think it."
—*Charles Dickens,* Bleak House

Two lawyers are partners. One day, when lunching together, the first lawyer suddenly says, "Damn! I've got to get back to the office."

"Why?" asks his partner.

"I forgot to lock the safe," he replies.

"So what does it matter," says the partner, "we're both here."

A lawyer and a physician were swimming at the seashore when they made a bet. They bet 25¢ as to who could hold their head under the water the longest. The lawyer drowned.

"Among attorneys in Tennessee the saying is: When you have the facts on your side, argue the facts. When you have the law on your side, argue the law. When you have neither, holler."

—*Albert Gore, Jr.*

Lawyers don't frequent nudist colonies. Nobody has pockets for them to put their hands into.

LAWYERS AND HOLLYWOOD

The most horrible and scariest of all *Friday the 13th* movies: "Jason Goes to Law School."

• •

When Heli-USA began a helicopter commuting service between Los Angeles–area airports for as much as $180 a day, Heli-USA's president noted that its clients are "mostly attorneys and people in the movie business."

• •

Fyvush Finkle in a 1995 episode of "Picket Fences":

"I'm the lawyer. Don't saddle me with the truth."

• •

Back to the Future III promises that one day lawyers will be outlawed.

• •

"You know, for a *lawyer* you're some good kisser."

—*Jane Fonda to Robert Redford,
in* Barefoot in the Park

••••••••••••••••••••••••••••••••

Over the July 4th weekend, *The Firm* replaced *Jurassic Park* as the largest grossing movie in America, thus proving what everyone already suspected: Lawyers are a lot scarier than dinosaurs.

—*James Gorman,* New York Times

••••••••••••••••••••••••••••••••

And now, a selection from "WKRP in Cincinnati":

VENUS FLYTRAP: I'm not gonna sit here and let her lie!

LAWYER: You have to. This is a court of law.

••••••••••••••••••••••••••••••••

When Steve Martin in *Planes, Trains, and Automobiles* pays $75 to get a cab from another passenger, he says, "You're a thief." "Close," answers the passenger, "I'm an attorney."

••••••••••••••••••••••••••••••••

"One minute you're an attorney, the next minute you're an imbecile."

"That's not a very long trip."

—*from* Regarding Henry

When Harrison Ford's young son was asked at his preschool what his father did, the boy replied, "My daddy is a movie actor, and sometimes he plays the good guy, and sometimes he plays the lawyer."

To help protect children from the poverty he had encountered upon running away from home at age 11, W. C. Fields willed that his estate be used for the founding of W. C. Fields College for Orphan Boys and Girls. It was never founded. The fees of those lawyers representing Fields's wife and Fields's mistress consumed almost the entire estate.

In August 1993, when the American Bar Association convened at the New York Hilton, scores of hecklers demonstrated outside. Someone among them was heard chanting:

"It's safe to walk the streets,
the muggers have left in fear,
because the ABA is here!"

QUESTION: How was the copper wire invented?
ANSWER: Two lawyers fighting over a penny.

At one of its parties in 1993, the Luzerne County (Pennsylvania) Bar Association insisted that no Miller beer brands be served because Miller had recently run a TV commercial that capitalized on lawyer bashing.

QUESTION: What's the difference between a lawyer and an onion?
ANSWER: You cry when you cut up an onion.

When the devil takes shape, it's under the pretense of a lawyer.
—*Spanish proverb*

A gentleman goes to an ethnic deli for lunch. On the menu are:

Calves brains $2.50/pound
Monkey brains $15.00/pound
Lawyer's brains $200.00/pound

"Why so much for the lawyer's brains?" he asks the waiter.

"Do you know how many lawyers it takes to get a pound of brains?!"

"In one respect at least the Martians are a happy people; they have no lawyers."
—*Edgar Rice Burroughs,*
A Princess of Mars, *1912*

QUESTION: What's the difference between a lawyer and a hooker?
ANSWER: A hooker doesn't keep screwing you after you're dead.

What do you say to a lawyer entering the courtroom with a beautiful woman on his arm?

"Hey, where'd you get that great tattoo?"

QUESTION: Why do lawyers have their offices on the top floors of high-rise office buildings?
ANSWER: Because hot air rises.

"Education is worth a whole lot. Just think—with enough education and brains the average man would make a good lawyer—and so would the average lawyer."

—*Gracie Allen*

"In 1698 Connecticut actually classed lawyers with common drunkards and limited their number to eleven in the whole colony. Rhode Island forbade them to be elected to their House of Deputies. Vermont publicly called them 'bandits.'"

—*J. R. Dolan*, The Yankee Peddlers of Early America, *1964*

After losing in the highest court of appeals, the defendant turned to his lawyer and said, "Where do we go from here?"

The lawyer looked him straight in the eyes and said, "What do you mean *we*? You go to prison, I go back to my office."

"Necessity knows no law; I know some attorneys of the same."
—*Benjamin Franklin*

Two guys are walking down the street and see a sign that says *Free Sex with Purchase of Legal Services*. They both go in and ask the lawyer to draw up their wills.

When the lawyer finishes, they ask about their free sex. The lawyer says there are conditions. "You have to guess the right number between 1 and 10."

The first guy says, "I guess 7." "Nope," says the lawyer, "the number was 2."

Then the second guy tries, "I guess 2." "Nope," says the lawyer, "this time the number was 5."

After the two guys leave the lawyer's office and continue on down the street, the one guy says, "Damn! That deal's rigged! It's a scam!"

"No, it isn't," says the other, "it's on the up and up. My sister has used that lawyer twice and she's won both times."

QUESTION: What's 12 inches long and hangs in front of an asshole?
ANSWER: A lawyer's tie.

Talk is cheap until you hire a lawyer.

Successfully defending his client in a lawsuit, the attorney presented him with an invoice. "You can pay $1,000 now," the lawyer said, "then $200 a month for the next 36 months."

"That sounds like buying a car," said the client.

The lawyer nodded, "I am."

—Parts Pups

"A lawyer with his briefcase can steal
more than a hundred men with guns."
—*Mario Puzo*

T-shirt spotted at Harvard Law School
commencement:
>Don't tell my Mom I'm a lawyer.
>She thinks I play piano
>in a whorehouse.

QUESTION: What's the difference between a rooster and a lawyer?

ANSWER: A rooster clucks defiant.

"Your Royal Majesty, Grafton County, New Hampshire, consists of 1,212 square miles. It contains 6,489 souls most of whom are engaged in agriculture, but included in that number are 69 wheelwrights, 8 doctors, 29 blacksmiths, 87 preachers, 20 slaves, and 90 students at the new college. There is not one lawyer, for which fact we take no personal credit but thank an Almighty and Merciful God."

>—*the 1770 census report of the County Clerk of Grafton County, New Hampshire, to King George III*

"There is no shortage of lawyers in Washington, D.C. In fact, there may be more lawyers than people."
—*Sandra Day O'Connor*

Two lawyers are walking through the woods when they spot a mean-looking bear. One lawyer immediately sits down, opens up his briefcase, pulls out a pair of sneakers, and starts to put them on.

"What are you doing?" asked the second lawyer. "You can't outrun a bear!"

"I don't have to. I only have to outrun you."

A handsome young man turned off a number of young ladies he met in a bar. "Listen," the bartender said, "don't tell them you're a plumber. These chicks want to meet professional men. Next time say you're a lawyer."

Moments later a woman sat next to the man and asked his occupation.

"Lawyer," he said.

"You must have many interesting cases to talk about," she replied. "Why don't we go up to my apartment and you can fill me in?"

Soon they were in bed and he was laughing. "Why are you laughing?" she asked.

"This is great. I've only been a lawyer for an hour and I'm already screwing somebody."

"I wouldn't write a song about any of them."

—*John Lennon, on lawyers*

It is interesting to note that criminals have multiplied of late, and lawyers have also; but I repeat myself.

A destitute man need have no fear of lawyers for the same reason he need have no fear of pickpockets.

—*Arabic proverb*

A city lawyer was walking down a country road when he saw a farmer plowing a field with a mule. Though there was only one mule, the farmer called out, "Faster, Bill! Get with it, Tom! Keep up the pace, Al! Work harder, Jim!"

The lawyer yelled over to the farmer, "Excuse me, but why are you calling that mule several different names?"

"He works harder," said the farmer, "if he thinks there's a bunch more mules workin' with him."

The lawyer went back to his office and invented the committee.

"Beware of the teachers of the law. They like to walk around in flowing robes and love to be greeted in the market-places and have the most important seats in the synagogues and the places of honor at banquets. They devour widows' houses . . ."

—*Luke 20:46–47*

"In both instances, you had a tremendous number of lawyers who fooled around and missed the main point. Isn't that a symbol of what happens when you've got all these lawyers running things?"

—*Charlie Peters, editor of* Washington Monthly, *on the Clinton administration blowing its first two Attorney General nominations*

When God realized the need to chastise mankind he created lawyers.

—*Hebrew teaching*

A policeman sees a young boy playing with garbage and asks him what he's doing.

"Building a policeman," says the boy.

"Why not build a lawyer," suggests the officer.

"Not enough garbage."

No lawyer shall ever enter Heaven as long as there is space in Hell.

—*Gaelic saying*

For a good time, hire a hooker,
For a lot of time, hire my attorney.
—*prison cell graffiti*

The devil makes his Christmas pie of lawyers' tongues.
—*English pub toast*

"They do tricks even I can't figure out."
—*Harry Houdini, on lawyers*

A chiropractor standing in line at a movie theater notices that the man in front of him has a bent and painful-looking back. He reaches forward, grabs the man's shoulders, and gives him a quick spinal adjustment.

The man turns around and screams, "What the hell are you doing!?"

"I was only trying to help," replied the chiropractor. "You looked so uncomfortable and I'm a chiropractor, and I was sure I could help by giving you an adjustment. It's what I do for a living."

"So!?" yelled the man, "I'm a lawyer. Do you see me screwing the man in front of me?"

DEAR ANN LANDERS

I have a problem. My mother was a prostitute. My father is in jail for selling drugs to children in the schoolyard. My sister is a junkie, and my brother is a lawyer. I am getting married to a wonderful girl. My question is this: should I tell her about my brother, the lawyer?

Involving lawyers in a dispute is comparable to giving drinks to an alcoholic. One is too many and a thousand are not enough.

Homicide, *n*., the slaying of one human being by another. There are four kinds of homicide: felonious, excusable, justifiable, and praiseworthy, but it makes no great difference to the person slain whether he fell by one kind or another—the classification is for advantage of the lawyers.

—*Ambrose Bierce,*
The Devil's Dictionary

QUESTION: How do you save a lawyer from being depressed?
ANSWER: Who cares?

It is hard to say whether the doctors of law or of divinity have made the greatest advances in the lucrative business of mystery.

"[Lawyers] have to twist themselves out of shape. They have to become more nasty and aggressive than they would normally be . . ."

—*anonymous psychoanalyst*

A fox may steal your hens, sir
If a lawyer's hand is fee'd, sir
He steals your whole estate.

—*John Gay,* The Beggar's Opera

A mobster was on trial, facing a possible life sentence, but his lawyer bribed a juror to hold out for a lesser charge. After hours of deliberation, the jury returned a verdict carrying a maximum of ten years in prison.

Afterward, the lawyer approached the juror. "You had me worried! When the jury was out so long, I was afraid you couldn't pull it off."

"I was worried too!" answered the juror. "The others all wanted to acquit him."

—*quoted on* WPEN, *Philadelphia*

"The reason that hookers practice the world's oldest profession is that in ancient times there were no bar exams to take."

—*Charles B. Sullivan*

34

A rabbi, a Hindu, and a lawyer were driving through the country when their car broke down. At a nearby farm, where they hoped to find a place to sleep for the night, only two beds were available. One of them would have to sleep in the barn. The Hindu volunteered.

Ten minutes later, there was a knock on the farmhouse door—it was the Hindu. "I am very sorry but I did not realize there was a cow in the barn. A cow is sacred to Hindus so I cannot sleep in this one's presence."

The rabbi then volunteered to sleep in the barn. Ten minutes later, there was a knock on the farmhouse door—it was the rabbi. "I am very sorry but I did not realize that there was a pig in the barn. As the pig is not kosher, I cannot sleep in the same room with one."

So the lawyer went to the barn to sleep. Ten minutes later there was a knock on the farmhouse door—it was the cow and the pig.

"If a boy has enough intelligence he should consider entering the ministry, unless when he goes to the university he is given to carousing, drinking, and wenching, in which case he ought to consider law."

—*J. Collyer, 1761*

A plant native to New Zealand, a climbing vine with yellow berries and very sharp thorns is known locally as the "bush lawyer" because of how difficult it is to escape from its thorns.

—Philadelphia Inquirer Magazine, *May 31, 1992*

"Lawyers have been known to wrest from reluctant juries triumphant verdicts of acquittal for their clients, even when those clients, as often happens, were clearly and unmistakably innocent."

—*Oscar Wilde*

A balloonist realizes that he is lost as he floats over the countryside. Seeing someone on the ground, he calls out, "I am lost. Can you tell me where I am?"

"Yes," replies the pedestrian, "you're in a balloon."

"You're an attorney, aren't you?" yells back the balloonist.

"Yes, how did you know?"

"For two reasons," says the balloonist. "First, what you told me was absolutely true. Second, it was absolutely worthless."

A blind rabbit and a blind snake met in the garden. The rabbit told the snake that since he was blind, he did not know what kind of animal he was.

The snake crawled around the rabbit and told him, "Well, you have long ears; your front legs are smaller than your rear legs, and you have a fluffy powder puff for a tail."

The rabbit then stated, "Gee, I am a rabbit."

Then the snake told the rabbit that he did not know what he was either, since he was blind. So the rabbit hopped around the snake and said, "You are low-down, slimy, and have a forked tongue."

The snake then exclaimed, "Oh my God, I'm a lawyer!"

God save us from a lawyer's etcetera.
—*French proverb*

"I used to be a lawyer, but now I am a reformed character."

—*Woodrow Wilson*

Question: What do lawyers and sperm have in common?
Answer: Only one in two million ever do anything worthwhile.

"Why are lawyers thought of so badly? Why are we found near the bottom of nearly every public opinion ranking of occupations? The answer is simple: Because we deserve it!"

—*Alan M. Dershowitz,*
Contrary to Popular Opinion

"If it weren't for wills, lawyers would have to work at an essential employment. There is only one way you can beat a lawyer in a death case. That is to die with nothing. Then you can't get a lawyer within ten miles of your house."

—*Will Rogers*

Some folks are never quite sure if it's better to tell the truth or hire a lawyer.

A stingy old lawyer was dying. His last wish was to prove wrong the old saying, "You can't take it with you." So he instructed his wife to fill up two pillow-cases with cash and place them in the attic directly over his bed. His plan was to grab the pillowcases as he passed by them on his way to heaven.

After the funeral, his widow checked the attic, only to find the cash still sitting there. "Oh that darn fool," she moaned, "I knew he should have put the money in the basement."

One way to cut back on the surplus of lawyers in this country is to stop letting them out on parole.

A doctor, a lawyer, and an anthropologist were on safari when they were captured by cannibals. The chief cannibal explained to the three that they would be that evening's dinner. "We will boil you, eat you, then use your skins to cover our canoes. However, as is our custom, I will grant each of you one last wish."

The doctor, thinking of the pain to be faced, requested a shot of morphine from his medical bag.

The anthropologist, familiar with hallucinogenics found in nature, asked if he could chew on the leaves of a specific plant.

And the lawyer requested a sharp stick. When his puzzled captors obliged, the lawyer immediately began to puncture the skin all over his body, declaring with great satisfaction, "So much for your damn canoes!"

"The minute you read something and you can't understand it, you can almost be sure that it was drawn up by a lawyer."

—*Will Rogers*

The U.S. Postal Service had to recall its commemorative series of stamps depicting famous lawyers. People were confused about which side to spit on.

HERE COMES THE JUDGE!

An Allegheny County, Pennsylvania, judge asked a male attorney to take off his jacket and then invited a female lawyer to "take off anything you want."

• •

A judge in Baltimore County, Maryland, granted probation to a man convicted of raping a drunken woman. The judge explained that, after all, an unconscious woman on a bed was "the dream of a lot of males, quite honestly."

• •

An Idabel, Oklahoma, judge released a man from jail after only three months because he had not used a gun against his wife. The man had, instead, beaten his wife to death.

• •

A judge in Jonestown, Pennsylvania, dismissed speeding charges against a fashion model who said she was being chased by four men. The judge went on to explain that he would have doubted her story if she had been "an ugly broad."

"Woe unto you also, ye lawyers! for ye lade men with burdens grievous to be borne, and ye yourselves touch not the burdens with one of your fingers."

—*Luke 11:46*

In 1990, Virginia's House of Delegates endorsed a bill authorizing the Board of Game and Inland Fisheries to establish a hunting and trapping season and bag limit on attorneys. The bill states "the board shall consider the proliferation of attorneys and their classification as a nuisance species." The bill offers some protection to lawyers. For example, sportsmen are not allowed to use currency as bait; or shout "whiplash," "ambulance," or "free scotch" for trapping purposes.

You can always tell a barber
By the way he parts his hair;
You can always tell a dentist
When you're in the dentist's chair;
And even a musician—
You can tell him by his touch;
You can always tell a lawyer,
But you cannot tell him much.

—anonymous

Appeal, *n.*, in law, to put the dice into the box for another throw.

—Ambrose Bierce,
The Devil's Dictionary

A cruise ship with 1,500 passengers, including 650 lawyers on board for a tax-free bar association meeting, is suddenly hijacked soon after leaving port. The hijackers read a detailed list of demands to the Coast Guard, threatening, "If our demands are not met by 5 P.M., we will *release* one lawyer every 15 minutes, until they are."

"The plaintiff and the defendant in an action at law are like two men ducking their heads in a bucket, and daring each other to remain longest under water."

—*Samuel Johnson*

"I don't believe man is woman's natural
enemy. Perhaps his lawyer is."
—*Shana Alexander*

Old lawyers never die, they just smell
that way.
—*Senator James "Pate" Philip,
Illinois State Senate President*

QUESTION: Do you know why they bury
lawyers 20 feet in the ground?
ANSWER: Deep down, they're nice guys.

THE LEGAL MIND AT WORK

"Judges lie, then lawyers lie, then clients lie."

> —*Alan Dershowitz, reported October 25, 1993*

"Lawyers don't lie."

> —*Alan Dershowitz, reported December 10, 1994*

A 1994 auto race for lawyers at Indiana University (Bloomington) used an ambulance for a pace car.

Ed showed little aptitude for the law and even less for public speaking, but neither handicap prevented him from pursuing a career as a criminal attorney. When, finally, the day came for him to argue his first murder case, Ed invited a colleague to attend the trial and listen to his closing arguments.

Halfway through his summation, Ed slipped a note to his attorney friend: "How am I doing?"

"Keep talking," the lawyer wrote back. "The longer you talk, the longer he lives."

"When there are too many lawyers, there can be no justice."

—*Lin Yutang*

St. Peter was questioning three married couples to see if they qualified for admittance to Heaven.

The first man, who had been a physician, he asked, "Why do you deserve to pass the Pearly Gates?"

"I was a good father," he answered.

"Yes," said St. Peter, "but you were such a drunk you even married a woman named Sherry. Sorry, but no admittance."

St. Peter then asked the next man, who had been a banker, the same question.

"I was good to my neighbors and family."

"That's true," said St. Peter, "but you were also such an awful glutton that you even married a woman named BonBon. No admittance."

At this point, the third man, who had been a lawyer, stood up and said, "Come on, Penny, let's get out of here."

God was taking a stroll through Heaven one day when he came upon a rather large hole in the clouds. He looked down and saw the Devil sitting there busily at work. God called down to the Devil, "Hey Devil, I want you to get this hole fixed right away."

The Devil looked up from his work and said, "Yeah, sure, right away."

The next day, at the same spot in the clouds, God again came across the hole. Again he yelled down at the Devil, "Hey, I thought you were going to fix that hole right away."

"Sure, God," the Devil said, "right away."

On the third day, the hole was still there. Sternly, God called down, "Devil, if you don't get this hole fixed immediately, I'm going to sue you!"

The Devil looked up at God and with a smirk responded, "Oh yeah? And just where are you gonna get a lawyer?"

"Don't forget, I'm at Skadden, Arps now. We pride ourselves on being assholes. It's part of the firm culture."

> —*former U.S. District Judge Susan Getzendanner, on her move to Skadden, Arps, Slate, Meagher & Flom*

"Lawyers use the law as shoemakers use leather; rubbing it, pressing it, and stretching it with their teeth, all to the end of making it fit their purposes."

> —*Louis XII of France*

"I decided law was the exact opposite of sex; even when it was good, it was lousy."

—*Mortimer Zuckerman*

"Lawyers are always more ready to get a man into troubles than out of them."

—*Oliver Goldsmith*

"Some people think about sex all the time, some people think about sex some of the time, and some people never think about sex: they become lawyers."

—*Woody Allen*

QUESTION: How do you get a lawyer out of a tree?
ANSWER: Cut the rope.

"'A conscience for hire,' as our peasants call lawyers."

—*Dostoevsky*

These [the lawyers] are the
  mountebanks of the State,
Who by the sleight of tongues can
  crimes create.

—*Daniel Defoe*

STUFF LAWYERS
LOVE TO WRITE!

To adopt a mutt in Middletown, Delaware—just to save the little fellow from destruction—the following must be signed.

Release

KNOW ALL PERSONS BY THESE PRESENTS, that the undersigned, for and in consideration of the animal adoption undertaken this date, have remised, released, and forever discharged, and by these presents do for themselves, their heirs, executors, and administrators, remise, release, and forever discharge the Kent County SPCA, their successors, assigns, heirs, executors, administrators, and employees, of and from all, and all manner of action and actions, cause and causes of actions, suits, debts, dues, sums of money, accounts, reckoning, bonds, bills, specialties, covenants, contracts, controversies, agreements, promises, variances, trespasses, damages, judgments, extents, executions, claims, and demands whatsoever, in law or in equity, which the undersigned ever had, now have or which their heirs, executors, or administrators, hereafter can, shall or may have for, upon or by reason of any matter, cause or thing whatsoever, from the beginning of the world to the date of these presents; and without limiting the generality of the foregoing for all claims, known or unknown, arising out of ownership and/or possession of the adopted animal, which the undersigned specifically acknowledge(s) may be infected with rabies or some other unknown infirmity.

This release is not intended to be, nor shall be deemed or construed to be, an admission of liability on the part of the Kent County SPCA.

IN WITNESS WHEREOF, we have hereunto set our hands and seals this ___ day of _____, 19___.

In the presence of:

_____   _____ (SEAL)
_____   _____ (SEAL)
_____   _____ (SEAL)
_____   _____ (SEAL)

QUESTION: What do you get when you cross the Godfather with a lawyer?
ANSWER: An offer you can't understand.

A man walked into a bar with his alligator and asked the bartender, "Do you serve lawyers here?"

"Sure do," replied the bartender.

"Good," said the man, "give me a beer and my 'gator will have a lawyer."

QUESTION: What is the difference between a catfish and a lawyer?
ANSWER: One is a scum-sucking bottom dweller, and the other is a fish.

"When the lawyers are through, what is there left? . . . Can a mouse nibble at it and find enough to fasten a tooth in?"
—*Carl Sandburg*

A tiger was following an elephant about the jungle, eating all his droppings.

"What the hell are you doing?" asked the elephant.

"I ate a lawyer earlier today," replied the tiger, "and I'm just trying to get rid of the taste."

The Pope and a lawyer died at the same instant and found themselves in the presence of St. Peter. "Follow me," said St. Peter, "and I'll show you to your rooms."

St. Peter led the pair up a resplendent bejeweled staircase, down a wide corridor, and through a solid gold door to reveal a lavish room with thick, plush carpet, damask wall covering, and a king-size bed with a down mattress. There was a balcony that overlooked lush green gardens, and a faint scent of lilac filled the room.

St. Peter looked at the lawyer and said, "This is your room." To the Pope, St. Peter said, "Follow me."

They retraced their steps, descended several flights of stairs, and walked along a small, dark passageway, until they came to a low, rough hewn wooden door. Behind the door was a small cell with a cold, stone floor, no window, and a wooden pallet for a bed.

"This is your room," St. Peter said to the Pope.

Bewildered and widely disappointed, the Pope asked, "Why is it that I, a prince of the Roman Catholic Church, must spend eternity in this dungeon, while that lawyer is afforded such luxury?"

"Remember," St. Peter answered, "this is Heaven. We have many Popes, but only one lawyer."

"Lawyers enjoy a little mystery, you know. Why, if everybody came forward and told the truth, the whole truth, and nothing but the truth straight out, we should all retire to the workhouse."

—*Dorothy L. Sayers*

QUESTION: What's the difference between a lawyer and God?
ANSWER: God doesn't think he's a lawyer.

A LEGAL BUSINESS CARD

Dewy, Cheatham & Howe
Attorneys at Law

"Castles in the air are the only property
you can own without the intervention
of lawyers."

—*J. Feidor Rees*

"I would like to see the time come when the massive hemorrhage of some of our best talents into the [field of] law will cease. . . . Our country is already sufficiently litigation-prone and legalistic. The over-supply of lawyers not only helps create its own demand but can get in the way of solving problems."

—*David Riesman*

"Lawyers spend a great deal of their time shoveling smoke."

—*Oliver Wendell Holmes, Jr.*

"It has been my experience that members of the legal profession are contributing substantially to the erosion of values and institutions on which our societies are based. In their quest for money and power, many lawyers seem to have forgotten their obligations."

—*Admiral Hyman G. Rickover*

THE BURBOT . . .

. . . is a big, ugly, slimy fish with the head of a catfish and the tail of an eel. According to the *Grand Rapids Press*, "The burbot goes by a number of names like dogfish, eelpout, spineless cat, and *lawyer*. The latter comes from its distinctive snaky look and its well-known propensity for gluttonous feeding and habit of aggressively biting anything."

The sheriff received a telephone call from a rancher: "Sheriff, you better get right out here. I just ran over three lawyers."

When the sheriff arrived at the ranch, there was no sign of the accident. "Where are the three lawyers?" he asked.

"I buried them," said the rancher.

"Are you sure they were dead?" asked the sheriff.

"Well, they were screaming and hollering when I buried them," replied the rancher, "but you know how those lawyers lie."

The louder the voice, the weaker the case.

A fellow walking through a cemetery came across a tombstone with the epitaph,

HERE LIES A LAWYER AND
AN HONEST MAN.

To which the fellow wondered, "How'd they get two guys in the same grave?"

Some years ago, an incompetent attorney lost a murder case which resulted in a death sentence by electrocution against his unfortunate client. On the fateful night, before the sentence was carried out, the prisoner was asked what his last wish was. His reply: "I'd like my lawyer to sit on my lap."

Law school test question in Torts:

If A steals a case of beer from P and drinks it, is A liable to P?

Once there was a case where the defendant was charged with maiming another by biting off the victim's ear.

The defense lawyer asked the witness, "Did you see him bite off the ear?"

"No," the witness replied, "I did not."

Instead of sitting down, the lawyer continued, "Then just what makes you think he bit off the ear?"

"Well, sir," the witness calmly replied, "I saw him spit the ear out."

An attorney, a Boy Scout, and a physician were flying in a small plane when the pilot announced engine trouble and suggested that the passengers bail out.

However, there were only two parachutes. The doctor suggested the Boy Scout take one of the parachutes because of his youth. The lawyer said, "Because I'm the brightest trial attorney in the country, I should certainly have a parachute." Whereupon he grabbed a parachute and jumped out of the plane.

"Don't worry," said the Boy Scout to the doctor, "the smartest attorney in the country just bailed out with my backpack."

Theologians often ponder on what day God created lawyers, and why couldn't he have also rested on that day?

The Easter Bunny, Santa Claus, a crooked lawyer, and an honest lawyer are sitting around a table with a $100 bill on it. When the lights suddenly go out, who grabs the money?

The crooked lawyer. All the others are figments of your imagination.

"Do you know how to save a drowning attorney?"
"No."
"Good!"

FROM "FILES OF THE EXPECTED"

The June 1995 *New York Times* reports that according to maître d's and restaurant owners, lawyers "tip poorly and have an air of confidence that can mutate into arrogance."

● ●

The National Law Journal recently commissioned a poll which determined that "nine out of ten parents would not want their child to grow up to be a lawyer."

"We [in California] are suing ourselves to death. We are legally the most expensive state of the 50. We add huge costs to our products and we don't add value."

—*Peter Ueberroth*

"From the very beginning, this was handled by the lawyers."
> —*a top adviser to President Clinton, explaining how the Whitewater affair spun so badly out of control*

"If law school is so hard to get through, how come there are so many lawyers?"
> —*Calvin Trillin*

May your life be filled with lawyers.
> —*Mexican curse*

LEGAL BILLS—LAWYERS AT THEIR CREATIVE BEST

A West Virginia lawyer recently billed his client for a 74-hour day, claiming 22 hours of travel and 52 hours of court time.

• •

Buried within a Boston law firm's $2.9 million bill for a two-year trial was $140,000 for heating and air conditioning.

• •

Likewise, a San Diego firm billed for "HVAC" (translation: "Heating, Ventilation, and Air Conditioning").

• •

On three different occasions, the same Los Angeles lawyer submitted billing for a 50-hour workday.

• •

The $13 million bill that a Phoenix firm submitted to a client included a $1 million charge for a database that had absolutely nothing to do with the client's litigation.

When a law firm was caught billing $245 per hour for "preparing closing room," the lawyers explained that this was a fee for "physically putting the offering documents on the table and making sure there were coffee and pencils in the room."

And a New Orleans firm charges $500 for its one-sentence letters.

But watch out! Law firms bill for the time it takes to explain why it billed for time spent billing.

QUESTION: What do you have when you have a lawyer buried up to his neck in sand?

ANSWER: Not enough sand.

A law school lecturer told a graduating class, "Three years ago, when asked a legal question, you could answer in all honesty, 'I don't know.'"

Now you can say with great authority, "It depends."

—*Pamela Karlan*

In the mid-1700s, while attending a meeting of the bar at the Boston Coffee House, John Adams took note, a little gloomily, that lawyers "swarm and multiply," and wondered if measures to limit their numbers might be necessary.

In January 1992, *Newsweek* reports in on how the foolishness of Washington lawyers continues to run wild: at an estimated cost of $18,000, twenty attorneys recently met for two hours to discuss the typeface and paper color of a lobbying document.

A physician went golfing one day and badly hooked his very first tee shot across several fairways.

Looking for his ball, he found a lawyer lying on the ground moaning in pain and screaming, "I'm a lawyer and I'm suing you for 5,000 dollars!!"

"But," said the physician, "I yelled 'fore!'"

"Fine," said the lawyer, jumping up and shaking the physician's hand, "I'll settle out of court for four."

"The system of justice, and most especially the legal profession, is a whorehouse serving those best able to afford the luxuries of justice offered to preferred customers. The lawyer, in these terms, is analogous to a prostitute. The difference between the two is simple. The prostitute is honest—the buck is her aim. The lawyer is dishonest—he claims that justice, service to mankind, is his primary purpose."

—*Florynce Kennedy*

"The fact that a lawyer advised such foolish conduct, does not relieve it of its foolishness."

—*Lucilius A. Emery*

QUESTION: How do you tell when a lawyer is well hung?

ANSWER: When it's difficult to get your finger between the rope and his neck.

"I have only two lawyers in all my kingdom, and when I get home I intend to hang one of them."

—*Peter the Great, upon visiting London where he was shocked by the number of lawyers in Westminster Hall*

"Those lawyers with Hah-vud accents are always thinking up new ways to take advantage of people."

—*Harry Truman*

They couldn't bury a recently deceased lawyer straight in the ground because he was so crooked. Instead, they screwed him in.

"Going to law is like skinning a new milk cow for the hide, and giving the meat to the lawyers."

—*Josh Billings*

QUESTION: Why are lawyers like nuclear weapons?

ANSWER: If one side has one, the other side has to get one. Once launched during a campaign, they can rarely be recalled. And when they land, they screw up everything forever.

"Lawyers on opposite sides of a case are like the two parts of shears; they cut what comes between them, but not each other."

—*Daniel Webster*

"It is an honorable calling that you have chosen. Some of you will soon be defending poor, helpless insurance companies who are constantly being sued by greedy, vicious widows and orphans trying to collect on their policies. Others will work tirelessly to protect frightened, beleaguered oil companies from being attacked by depraved consumer groups."

> —*Art Buchwald,*
> *commencement address,*
> *Tulane University School of*
> *Law*

May you have a lawsuit in which you know you are right.

> —*Spanish gypsy curse*

A judge had appointed two young lawyers to defend an old, experienced horse-thief. After inspecting his counsel some time in silence, the prisoner rose in his place and addressed the bench.

"Air them to defend me?"

"Yes, sir," said the judge.

"Both of them?" asked the prisoner.

"Both of them," responded the judge.

"Then I plead guilty," and the poor fellow took his seat and sighed heavily.

—*Eli Perkins*

"You cannot live without lawyers, and certainly you cannot die without them."

—*Joseph H. Choate*

"Those who think the information brought out at a criminal trial is the truth, the whole truth and nothing but the truth, are fools. Prosecuting or defending a case is nothing more than getting to those people who will talk for your side, who will say what you want said."

—*F. Lee Bailey*

"Just when I thought there was no way to stop the Japanese from steadily widening their lead over American industry, I saw a headline in the paper that said Japan to Open Its Door to American Lawyers.

"That ought to do it."

—*Calvin Trillin*

It is better to be a mouse in a cat's mouth than a man in a lawyer's hands.
—*proverb*

"I think the law is really a humbug and a benefit principally to lawyers."
—*Henry David Thoreau*

"The practice of law in most courtrooms today is about as modern as performing surgery in a barbershop."
—*Gordon D. Schaber*

A BAD YEAR

In 1988, Baker & McKenzie became the first law firm to employ over 1,000 lawyers.

"In a body where there are more than one hundred talking lawyers, you can make no calculation upon the termination of any debate and frequently, the more trifling the subject, the more animated and protracted the discussion."
—*Franklin Pierce, on Congress*

". . . anthropologists of the next generation will look back in amazement . . . the most ambitious and brightest were siphoned off the productive work force and trained to think like a lawyer."

—*Washington Monthly*

"The accused presented the best witnesses that money could buy."

—*Oscar Wilde*

". . . the Pharisees and lawyers rejected the counsel of God. . . ."

—*Luke 7:30*

A lawyer's ink writes nothing until you have thrown silver into it.

—*Estonian proverb*

"Like most corporate attorneys, he sat squarely on the fence with both ears to the ground."

—*anonymous*

"I must be a great lawyer, and to be a great lawyer, I must give up my chance of being a great man."

—*André Maurois*

When the investment firm Drexel, Burnham, Lambert, Inc. faced charges from the Securities and Exchange Commission, it secured 115 lawyers to prepare its case; the SEC could afford only 15.

When in 1988, a man was arrested in New York for impersonating a lawyer, one judge noted, "I should have suspected he wasn't a lawyer. He was always so punctual and polite."

LAWYERS AND
BANK ROBBERS

"The line between a bank robber and a lawyer is a very thin one, anyway. In robbing a bank I always planned the job carefully, leaving nothing to chance. It's the same thing in trying a case. "Preparation is everything," lawyers say. Once you're inside the bank, you have to see everything, guard yourself against everybody. While he is putting in his case, the lawyer has to be equally alert, equally on guard against anything the other side might throw at him. In both professions, it helps to be a little paranoid.

"And whatever they might say in the law schools, it also helps to have a grudge against society. The criminal attacks society head on; the lawyer is trying to set you free after you have been caught so that you can go out and steal some more. Whether he succeeds or not, he profits from your crime. The only way you can pay him is out of the money you have got away with at one time or another, everybody knows that. It isn't called his share of the loot, of course. It's called "the fee." But that's only because he has a license that entitles him to do what he's doing, and you haven't."

—*Willie Sutton, bank robber*

Come, you of the law, who can talk if you please

Till the man in the moon will allow it's a cheese.

—*Oliver Wendell Holmes, Sr.*

In 1957, when Charles S. Rhyne, president of the ABA, proposed the founding and celebration of "Law Day," he was told by one member of the White House staff that President Eisenhower wouldn't sign anything glorifying lawyers.

"A commencement speech is a particularly difficult assignment. You're given no topic and are expected to inspire all the graduates with a stirring speech about nothing at all. I suppose that is why so many lawyers are asked to be commencement speakers."

—*Sandra Day O'Connor*

As a young man was walking down the street, he observed an extremely long funeral procession, a casket followed by a line of people that stretched for blocks. Surely, he thought, the deceased must be a very important person.

Determined to identify the deceased, he boldly approached the lady who was first in line behind the casket, and inquired as to who the dead person was.

"My lawyer," she said.

"What happened to him?" he asked.

"My pit bull attacked and killed him," she explained.

That's horrible, thought the young man as he continued to walk with the lady. Soon, however, he got to thinking about his recent divorce. And the house he no longer owned. And Congress.

He again turned to the lady and asked, "Might I be able to borrow your pit bull?"

She shrugged, pointed her thumb back over her shoulders, and said, "Get in line."

"I think we may class the lawyer in the natural history of monsters."

—*John Keats*

"First I charge a retainer; then I charge a reminder; next I charge a refresher; and then I charge a finisher."

—*Judah P. Benjamin, lawyer and Confederate statesman*

QUESTION: Why does a woman mail out perfumed, erotic valentines signed "Guess who?" to the home addresses of over 2,000 married men?

ANSWER: She's a divorce lawyer.

When a wealthy and elderly man's time was near, he demanded that his two lawyers be brought to his room.

When the lawyers arrived he told each to stand on opposite sides of his bed. Once the two lawyers were in place, the old man softly rested his head on the pillow, crossed his hands upon his chest, smiled, and said nothing.

After nearly 20 minutes of silence, the bolder of the two lawyers finally said, "Sir, you called for us. Now that we're here, what is it that you wish us to do?"

"Well," the dying man said, "you know I've always been a good Christian, attempting to pattern my life after that of Jesus. So I think that it's only fitting that when I go, I die like Jesus—between two thieves."

"The legal mind chiefly consists in illustrating the obvious, explaining the self-evident and expatiating on the commonplace."

—*Benjamin Disraeli*

"America has one hundred and ten million population, 90 percent of which are lawyers, yet we can't find two of them who have not worked at some time or another for an oil company. There has been at least one lawyer engaged for every barrel of oil that ever come out of the ground."

—*Will Rogers*

"I'll tell you what my daddy told me after my first trial. I asked him, 'How did I do?' He paused and said, 'You've got to guard against speaking more clearly than you think.'"

—*Howard Baker Jr.*

"Bar associations are notoriously reluctant to disbar or even suspend a member unless he has murdered a judge downtown at high noon, in the presence of the entire committee on Ethical Practices."

—*Sydney J. Harris*

Three cardiac patients being prepared for their heart transplants are able to choose their donors. The first patient chooses the heart of an athlete for surely it will be a healthy heart.

The second patient chooses the heart of a priest for it will be a good and moral heart.

And finally, the third patient chooses the heart of a lawyer. Quite puzzled, his surgeon asks him why, for no one has ever before chosen a lawyer's heart. "It's quite simple," said the patient, "I want one that's never been used before."

It's frightening to think about putting one's fate in the hands of 12 people who weren't even smart enough to get out of jury duty.

"Almost all legal sentences, whether they appear in judges' opinions, written statutes or ordinary bills of sales, have a way of reading as though they had been translated from the German by someone with a rather meager knowledge of English. Invariably they are long. Invariably they are awkward. Invariably and inevitably they make plentiful use of the abstract, fuzzy, clumsy words which are so essential to the solemn hocus-pocus of the Law."

—*Fred Rodell,*
Woe Unto You, Lawyers!

"A new firm is successful when it has more clients than partners."

—*Henny Youngman*

"We [lawyers] shake papers at each other the way primitive tribes shake spears."

—*John Jay Osborn Jr.*

The only difference between a lawyer and a buzzard is that the lawyer takes off his wing tips at night.

"The trouble with lawyers is they convince themselves that their clients are right."

—*Charles W. Ainey*

An oil company hired three men at the same time. One was a geologist, one an engineer, and the third, a lawyer. Eventually only one was to be promoted.

A plan was devised to determine which of the three would receive the promotion. Each would be asked the exact same question, and depending on the answer, the promotion decision would be made.

The geologist was asked, "What is 3 plus 2?" He replied, "Somewhere between 4 and 6."

The engineer was asked the same question. He answered, "It can't be anything but 5."

Then the question was posed to the lawyer. He thought about it for a few seconds then leaned over to the interviewer and asked, "What do you want it to be?"

In 1522, Emperor Charles V officially directed the conqueror Cortés to expel all lawyers from New Spain so as to keep down the number of lawsuits.

"A rattlesnake bit a lawyer on the chin. The lawyer is recovering but the rattlesnake died."

—*from an episode of "Bonanza"*

WORD PLAY

Pettifogger, *n.*, an inferior lawyer.

An overpersistent insurance solicitor followed W. C. Fields into a barbershop. Fields finally exploded, "I've told you 'no' ten times now. Just to shut you up, I'll put your proposition up to my lawyer the next time I see him."

"Will you take the proper step," persisted the solicitor, "if he says it's okay?"

"I certainly will," asserted Fields, "I'll get another lawyer."

"For every man in prison there is an attorney out there who represented him."

—*"The Wizard of Id"*
cartoon caption

A lawyer walks into a doctors office with a toad sitting on his head.

Doctor says, "What can I do for you?"

The toad says, "How about cutting this wart off my ass."

QUESTION: How many lawyer jokes really exist?

ANSWER: Just three. The rest are true stories.

CONTRIBUTORS

Margie C. Angle, 45b

Anonymous at contributor's request, 10d, 32a, 53a, 85a

Joseph Arends, M.D., 5b

Syd Askoff, 83a

Diane Baker, 31a

Walter Ball Jr., 102a

W. L. Berry, 7a, 17b, 74b, 75a, 100a

Roderick M. Boyes, 9a

Hap M. Butler, 9c, 10a

Frank S. Cambensy, 8a

Jack Carroll, 74a

Richard A. Chambers, 56a

Andrew C. Clarke, 36a

Lawrence S. Cohen, M.D., 68a

Tom Copenhauer, 15b

Gary S. Dawson, 6b, 68b, 69a

Glen H. Deem, 66a

Theunis Dey, 22a

John A. Dowling, 43b

Dan Downing, 28b

Ejembi Eko, 33c, 45a

Pete Engel, 100b

Miguel Angel Fernández D., 14c

Phillip Fredrickson, 50a

Jerry Glader, 38a

Neil B. Goodhue, 8b

Michael Gray, 18a, 18c

Alane Greiner-Knudson, 15a

Charles E. Griffin II, 78b

Greg Groninger, 58c

Daniel L. Gwinn, 31b

Linda A. Hall, 34a

William J. Haltigan, 36b

Channing F. Hayden Jr., 24a, 75b

D. G. Taylor Hemple, 71b

Damon C. Hopkins, 39b

David E. Jerome, 37b

Kelly Kingston, 13b

Richard S. Kwieciak, 66b, 67a

Michael J. Laird, 58a, 58b, 62b

Rodney John Lamplugh, 20b

William J. Luecke, 73d

Michael MacLean, 77a

Myrlene Marsa, 35a

Judy Martin, 101b

Edward Meredith, 59b

Louis P. Michelin, 98b

Charles G. Milden, 16c

David Mokotoff, 96a

Bob Nichilo, 47a

Jack B. Osborne, 99a

Gail Packard, 102b

Abigail Packard-Rapp, 11d

Elaine C. Paral, 20a

George R. Peacock, 48c

Richard L. Pearse Jr., 60a

Senator James "Pate" Philip, 48b

Jeffrey R. Portko, 64b

Neilson F. Powell, 93a

Dolly Reinhold, 10c, 11c

GET YOUR NAME IN A BOOK! (MAYBE AGAIN!) SHOW IT OFF TO FRIENDS AND RELATIVES!

• •

Submit your favorite lawyer item—quotation, anecdote, court testimony, joke, lie, et cetera—for possible publication in *Lawyers and Other Reptiles III: The Rebuttal*. If the submission is used, you will receive credit and a free copy of the new book. Don't tell your lawyer about this—the snake'll charge you just for listening. Your submission will **not** be accepted if it is on legal-sized paper. And to ensure that no material is ever repeated, be sure that you've also purchased (multiple copies are encour-

107

aged!) and reviewed the original *Law-yers and Other Reptiles*. Submit to:

Lawyers and Other Reptiles III:
The Rebuttal
Attention: Jess M. Brallier
c/o Contemporary Books, Inc.
Two Prudential Plaza
Chicago, Illinois 60601-6790

Until then.